Lists

EASY WORD ESSENTIALS 2019

BOOK 3

M.L. HUMPHREY

SELECT TITLES BY M.L. HUMPHREY

WORD ESSENTIALS 2019

Word 2019 Beginner

Word 2019 Intermediate

EASY WORD ESSENTIALS 2019

Text Formatting

Page Formatting

Lists

Tables

Track Changes

CONTENTS

Introduction   1

Bulleted Lists   3

Numbered Lists   9

Multilevel Lists   17

Conclusion   25

Appendix A: Basic Terminology   27

About the Author   29

Introduction

The *Easy Word Essentials 2019* series of books is designed for those users who just want to learn one specific topic rather than have a more general introduction to Microsoft Word 2019, which is provided in *Word 2019 Beginner* and *Word 2019 Intermediate*.

Each book in this series covers one specific topic such as formatting, tables, or track changes.

I'm going to assume in these books that you have a basic understanding of Microsoft Word. However, this book does include an appendix with basic terminology just in case I use a term that isn't familiar to you or that isn't used the way you're used to.

This entire series of books is written for users of Word 2019. If you have a different version of Word then you might want to read the *Easy Word Essentials* series instead which is written as a more general approach to learning Microsoft Word.

For most introductory topics there won't be much of a difference between the two, but just be aware that this particular series does not worry about compatibility with other versions of Word whereas the more general series does.

Also, just a reminder that the content of this book is directly pulled from *Word 2019 Beginner* and/or *Word 2019 Intermediate* so there may be references in the text that indicate that.

Alright. Now that the preliminaries are out of the way, let's discuss lists.

Bulleted Lists

A bulleted list is just what it sounds like, a list of items where each line starts with some sort of marker or bullet on the left-hand side. The most common bullet choice is probably a small dark black circle that's filled in, but Word has additional options you can choose from such as an open circle, a filled-in square, and a checkmark. (See image below.)

You can either start a bulleted list before you have your items ready or you can take a list of items, highlight them, and then apply a bulleted list.

With either option, the way to do this is to go to the Paragraph section of the Home tab and click on the arrow next to the bulleted list option to bring up a dropdown menu where you can select the type of bullet you want.

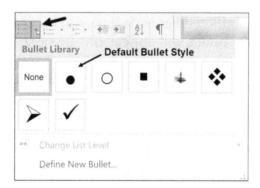

If you simply click on the image of the bulleted list instead of using the dropdown menu, your bullet will be a solid black circle.

Here are samples of each of the bullet choices shown above. (I had to create this by going into each line and choosing a different bullet type for that line. The default with bulleted lists is that once you choose a bullet that will be the bullet used for every line.)

- Item 1
○ Item 2
▪ Item 3
┼ Item 4
❖ Item 5
➢ Item 6
✓ Item 7

When you choose to insert a bulleted list, if you don't have any text selected already then a single bullet will appear on the page where your cursor was, waiting for you to type in your first entry.

If you do have items selected, each paragraph will be indented and the bullet type you chose will be added at the beginning of each of the paragraphs.

The mini formatting menu also has the bulleted list option available in the middle of the bottom row, so that's another option for applying or removing a bulleted list.

Once you've started a bulleted list each time you hit enter at the end of the text for a bulleted entry a new bullet will appear on the next line for you to add your next item.

Hit enter twice to return to normal paragraph indenting with no bullet. If you add a new bulleted list and then don't type any text before you hit enter again that will also revert back to no bullet.

(The double enter trick works for the first level of bullets. If you have a list with multiple levels of bullets, which we're about to cover, then you will need to hit enter until Word works its way through the levels of bullets and back to a blank option.)

You can create a bulleted list with multiple levels by using the Tab key to indent any line you want to the next level. Like so:

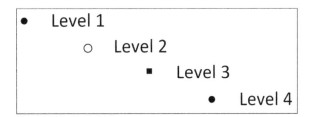

Here I've created three levels of indented text. I started with my first bullet and typed my text, then hit enter after Level 1. Next I used the tab to move that solid bullet in one level and create a second-level bullet. I then typed my text for that level and hit enter. And then repeated the process of tab, type, enter to create the other levels.

By default, when you hit enter from an existing line of a bulleted list the next line will be indented at that same level and will use the bullet mark for that level of indent.

To decrease an indent one level you can use Shift- + Tab.

When using Tab or Shift + Tab, if that line already has text in it be sure to place your cursor before any text. In the examples above, that would mean place it to the left of the first L in Level.

When you create a multi-level bulleted list, Word assigns a different bullet type for each indented level.

From what I can tell it uses the open circle for the first indented bullet, the black square for the second one, and then the black circle for the third one regardless of which option you chose for your first bullet. (See above.)

It then starts over again with the open circle for the next-level indent.

To change the bullet style for any level in your list, click on that line and go to the bulleted list options and choose a new bullet type.

That will apply that new bullet type to all lines in your list that are indented at that level. So, for example, all second-level indents will have the same bullet type and if you change that type for one line it will change it for *all* second-level indents in your list even if they are not listed together.

To remove bullets from a list, select the list, and then click on the bulleted list option in the Home tab or mini formatting menu. Your bullets will be removed, but the text will remain indented.

Another option for removing a bullet is to go to the beginning of the text for that line and backspace. Once will remove the bullet but keep the text where it is. Twice will move the text to the beginning of the line.

(You can also use the Format Painter to apply bullets to a list of entries or to remove them.)

With bulleted lists, Word will automatically indent your bullet and text when it adds the bullet for the first level. If you don't want that, you can use the Decrease Indent option to move the bullet back to the left-hand side of the page but keep the bullets.

If you decrease the indent for the first level of a multi-level bulleted list, this moves all levels back one indent.

The same works for increasing the indent using the Home tab option. If you increase the indent for the first level, it will increase the indent for all levels.

(For levels below that first level using Decrease Indent or Increase Indent just moves that specific line forward or backward one indent.)

You can also use the Paragraph dialogue box to have more control over how much each line is indented and whether each bulleted line should be treated as a hanging paragraph or not.

Another option you can use for indenting is the Adjust List Indents option from the dropdown menu on the main workspace. That will bring up the Adjust List Indents dialogue box.

This dialogue box allows you to choose the indent amount for the bullet. (It also is available for numbered lists, which we'll talk about next.)

The first choice is how much to indent the bullet or number.

The second choice is how much to indent the associated text.

The third choice is what type of separator to use between the bullet or number and the text. The default is a tab but you can also choose to use a space or nothing.

The choices you make here are probably more finicky for numbered lists than they are for bulleted lists since the bullet size remains constant no matter how many entries you have in your list. With numbered lists you have to move from 1 through 9 to 10 to 99 and then to 100 on which requires different amounts of space so each change can create a difference in the appearance of the list.

One more thing to note and then we'll move on to numbered lists.

I often will use the Paragraph dialogue box to add extra line spacing between bulleted list entries since sometimes I think entries in a list look better with a little more spacing between them than is used in a normal paragraph.

Numbered Lists

A numbered list is similar to a bulleted list except the entries are either labeled with numbers or letters. If you've ever had to provide an outline of a paper for school, I'm sure you've run across a numbered list before.

One easy way to create a numbered list is to simply type the first number you want to use, the separator mark you want, and then a space.

So, for example, if I type a capital A and then a period and then a space that will give me the first entry in a numbered list that uses A, B, C, D, etc.

When I do that, Word automatically indents that text and turns it into the first entry in a numbered list so that when I type in my text and then hit enter the next line will be "numbered" in sequence and indented as well.

(If Word ever does that to you and you don't want it to indent and start creating a list, just use Ctrl + X to Undo. You can also click on the little AutoCorrect dropdown that appears to the left-hand side of the entry and choose to undo from there.)

The other option, especially if you already have your text entered and just need to convert it to a numbered list, is to select the lines you want to number, go to the Paragraph section of the Home tab, click on the arrow next to the Numbering option, and choose the numbered list option you want from there.

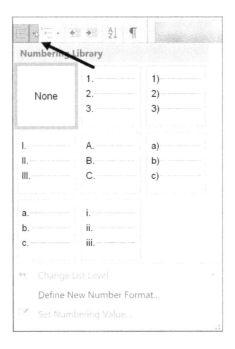

As you can see, you have the option to choose between lists that use

1, 2, 3

i, ii, iii

I, II, III

A, B, C

a, b, c

and then between using a period (.) or a paren( )) as the separator.

For a basic list, that should be all you really need. The default numbering choice if you just click on the image instead of using the dropdown is 1, 2, 3 separated with a period.

(In addition to the Home tab, the mini formatting menu also has the numbered list option.)

As with bulleted lists, you can create a multi-level list by using the tab key to indent a line or paragraph in your numbered list, but there appears to be that same pre-defined order for what will be used for each of the indented levels.

For the first indent Word uses the lower-case letters (a, b, c). For the second indent it uses lower-case Roman numerals (i, ii, iii). For the third indent it uses regular numbers (1, 2, 3). And then it cycles through again starting with the fourth-level indent. Like so:

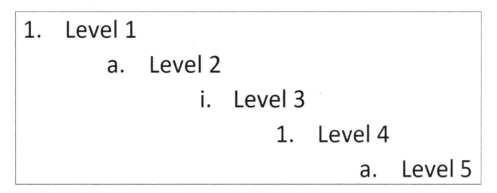

This generally results in a multi-level list that doesn't fit what I was taught in school which was I, A, 1, a, i for the numbering order for different levels.

To create a list with customized numbering in each level, you'd need to use the Multilevel List option which we are not covering here because it has given me more problems over the years than probably anything else I've ever worked with in Word.

(It's the option to the right of the number list option in the Paragraph section if you want to experiment with it and I do reluctantly cover it in *Word 2019 Intermediate.*)

For now, back to basic numbered lists.

If you had a numbered list earlier in your document and want that numbering to continue with additional numbered items later in your document, you can do that. Likewise if Word continued the numbering and you didn't want it to, you can change the settings to restart the numbering.

In either case, create your numbered list and then right-click on the number for the line you want to change.

Depending on what else is in your document and which entry you click on, you will see different options in the dropdown menu.

Restart at 1 or Restart at A will change the number of the entry to 1 or A or whatever the first value would be for that numbering type. All you have to do is click on this one for it to be applied.

Continue Numbering is also applied immediately. Click on it to continue the numbering from the last time that numbering type was used. So if you have a list in your document that has the "numbers" A, B, C and another list that has numbering of 1 and 2 and the numbering style on your current line is the A, B, C style then when you choose to continue numbering your next entry will be D even if the 1 and 2 values are closer to that line in the document.

(If it sounds confusing, just play around with it in Word and you'll see what I'm talking about.)

The final option you'll see is Set Numbering Value which will bring up the Set Numbering Value dialogue box when you choose it.

This gives you the most control over what happens with your list numbering. You can restart the list, continue numbering, continue numbering with skipped numbers, or start numbering at any value you want.

If you do set the numbering at a random value, just be aware that your choices are based upon the list type for that line. So if it's a level that's numbered with Roman numerals then you'd have to use X for 10, you couldn't type in 10.

Be a little careful with all of this because a change to the numbering style of one entry will change all other linked lines which is great when that's what you want but can be dangerous if you're working with a very large document and don't realize that the list on page fifty is somehow tied into the list on page ten.

Always if you're working with numbered lists be sure to go back through your entire document at the end to make sure that a change you made towards the end of the document didn't change something at the beginning of the document.

(This actually goes for page or section breaks as well. Best practice is to always do one last read through or scan of a document after all changes have been made and to restart that scan from the beginning if you end up making more changes.)

Okay. A few final points. As with bulleted lists you can change the indent and format of your numbered list using the Paragraph dialogue box or the Adjust List Indents option on the dropdown menu.

Also, I mentioned it above, but one thing to be careful of with numbered lists that go into the double-digits or triple-digits is that you can end up with a situation where the text is lined up for values of 1 through 9 but then not aligned once you reach a value of 10 or more.

This can happen, for example, when you use a space instead of a tab to follow the number, but I want to say that I've also seen it happen with tabs if the tabs were set in such a way that it changed which tab stop was used for 1 through 9 versus 10.

Also, it won't be an issue most times, but if you hold your mouse over the numbered list options that Word gives you by default some are right-aligned and some are left-aligned. As you move into larger and large values for your numbered list this may impact the appearance of your list.

To fix this, you'll need to create a New Number Format where you can customize the alignment. That option is at the bottom of the dropdown menu under Define New Number Format. (See screenshot on next page.)

Click on that and it will bring up the Define New Number Format dialogue box where you can choose the number style, number format (whether to use a period or paren or something else even), and the number alignment.

So, for example, the default for 1,2,3 is left-aligned. But you could use this option to make it right-aligned or centered. Here are what those three options look like for numbered values of 9 and 10:

> 9.　Level 1 Left-Aligned
> 10.　Level 2 Left-Aligned
>
>
> 9.　　Level 1 Centered
> 10.　　Level 2 Centered
>
>
> 9.　　Level 1 Right-Aligned
> 10.　Level 2 Right-Aligned

The only change I made here is in the alignment of the numbers. You can see in the first example that the 9 lines up with the 1 in 10. In the second sample it lines up with the center of the 10. And in the third example it lines up with the 0 in the 10. Personally I prefer the right-aligned version. But the default is left-aligned, so the only way to get this is to create your own number format using Define New Number Format.

One nice thing in Word is that once you've used a number format in a document that format is available for you to select again in the Document Number Formats section in the Numbering dropdown menu of the Home tab or the mini formatting menu.

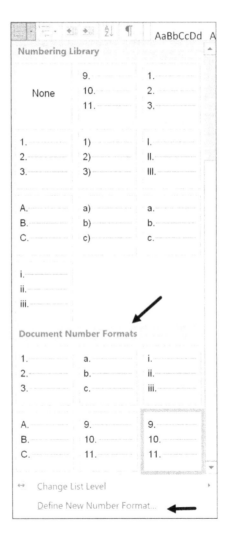

Although one weird thing about that section is that it will show formats you've used at one point but are no longer using. For example, in this screenshot I only have numbered lists in my document right now but it's showing lists with a, b, c, and A, B, C, and I, II, III even though they're not currently in use anywhere in the document.

(One of the reasons I'm careful with playing around with lists in a working document.)

In the case above where I had three different number formats for the 1, 2, 3 numbering you can't tell which is which just from looking. You have to hold your mouse over each one to figure out which one has each alignment.

You could also click on a line that already has that format and see which one of the formats in the dropdown is then surrounded by a dark gray border.

Or you could just use the Format Painter to copy the number formatting over, which is probably what I would actually do instead.

Multilevel Lists

Multilevel lists let you construct a custom outline format for use in your document. In school we were always told to outline with I, II, III as the first level, A, B, C as the second level, 1, 2, 3 as the third level, and a, b, c as the fourth level of an outline.

I have also worked for at least one employer who took this even a step further and mandated not just a specific order of how points and subpoints were to be numbered, but also specified by exactly how much each level needed to be indented on the page.

For that employer, most employees tried to use the standard numbered list option and it didn't work. So every single report we ever prepared someone (me) had to go through the report and "fix" it. The way to fix it was to create a customized multilevel list and then apply it throughout the document.

This could have changed in recent versions of Word, but I will say that having your custom multilevel list in place in a blank document before you ever begin is the best way to work with these lists.

I highly recommend that you create at least one example of each level you need before you ever type any other word in your document because trying to to do so after the fact is...a challenge.

So how do you create a multilevel list?

The easiest option is to use one of the pre-formatted choices that Word provides. None of them are exactly what I've needed in the past, but they can at least get close to what you need and if you're not as particular as my former employers or teachers, then using one of the existing lists is the simplest way to approach things.

I count seven possible choices. To see them, go to the Paragraph section of the Home tab and click on the dropdown for Multilevel List. You will get this:

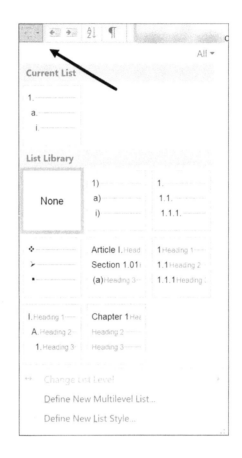

The closest one to what I described before looks like this when used:

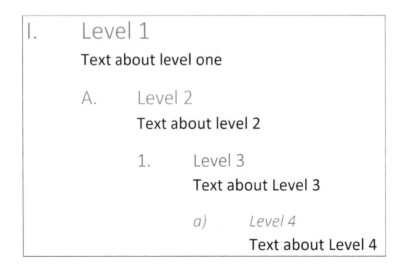

That almost works for me. I'd want to change the a with a paren for the last level to an a with a period. But the rest of it works, even those indents which are each an extra .5" per level.

Now one thing to note here with multilevel lists is that they are structured to allow text below each level.

See above where I have "Text about level..." under each of the numbered levels? I didn't have to remove a numbered value to do that. That's the default for how it works with a multilevel list (which is different from how it works with a bulleted or numbered list.) You have a numbered level, hit enter, and the next line is NOT numbered automatically when using a multilevel list.

So to get what you see above...

I went into my document, clicked on multilevel list and selected the list I wanted.

I then typed in the text for that level ("Level 1" for the first one) and hit enter.

The cursor for the next line started all the way back at the far left side of the page. To line that text up under Level 1 instead, I used tab and then typed my text ("Text about level one") and hit enter again.

At that point because I wanted another numbered level, I went back to the multilevel list dropdown menu and clicked on my list style that I had already chosen from the Current List section.

(Be careful that you don't end up running two separate lists within the same document. You can, but it may cause you lots of grief trying to keep numbering throughout your document consistent.)

Since I'd indented the line above, Word inserted an indented numbered list item that started with A. for me automatically.

I repeated the same process of adding text, enter, tab to indent, add more text, enter, and then add next list level until I had what you see above.

To change the level of a numbered line (so a line that's numbered II becomes an A or a 1 becomes a B) use the tab or shift + tab keys. You need to click onto the document right at the beginning of the text on that line (so right before the word Level in this example) and then tab will increases the indent one level, shift + tab will decrease the indent one level.

Word does not enforce any sort of hierarchical integrity. Meaning you can go from I to the next line being a) and skip right over A and 1 and Word won't do anything to warn you or prevent that. So if you're using an outline in a large document, you need to pay attention to where you are in your outline.

One way to do that is to use the Headings view in the Navigation pane. (Use Ctrl + F for find is an easy way to make it appear if it isn't already visible.) Because the other thing about the default multilevel lists is they also want to assign a heading style to each entry. (Which also means that another way to assign a level to a line within your document once you've started using a multilevel list is to assign that heading level style to that line.)

Okay. That was basic multilevel lists. Here's the ugly part: Changing one of those levels to what you want.

This is something I always struggle to get right because for some reason it always breaks some other part of my document.

For example, I mentioned above that I want that fourth level to use a period instead of a paren. You'd think you could just go in and change that one little line to be what you want and it would work. But I personally have never been able to get that to work for me. It's like squeezing a balloon. I get one part of it working and something else squishes out of shape on me.

So what I do is use the Define New Multilevel List option instead. Clicking on that option brings up the Define New Multilevel List dialogue box.

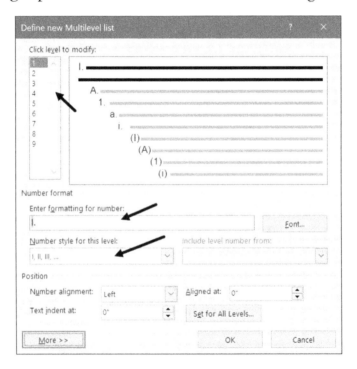

Choose each level by clicking on the number for the level on the top left.

Next, select the numbering style you want from the second dropdown menu in the number format section (I, II, III, or A, B, C, etc.).

Once you have your numbering style you can go right above that and change the format for that number to use a paren or period or whatever you want.

To do this, click into the box and add or delete what you need.

As you make these changes, the preview section in the top of the dialogue box will change to show your edits so you have an idea what the document will look like with the changes you've made.

So in the image above I've created a numbered list where it goes I, A, 1, a, i with periods first and then parens second and you can see that in the preview section.

Next, click on More in the bottom left corner and make sure that your changes are going to be applied to your whole document. (As I said before, you can have multiple lists in a document but it's problematic to do so.)

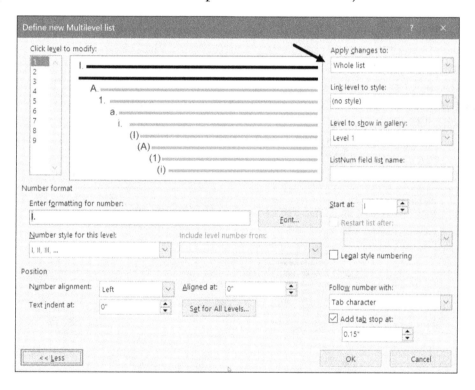

Word's help suggests that you give the list a name in the ListNum Field List Name field on the right-hand side of the top section as well and that if you want your list to use an existing style from your document you can change the Link Level to Style dropdown choice to select that style.

For every level except for the first level, make sure that the Restart List After option is checked and that the name of the prior level is showing in that dropdown box. That way if you had a point 1 with three subpoints and you're now on point 2 and it also has a subpoint that subpoint will be numbered a and not d.

The next step is to set your indents for your text and your numbers.

Let's use that employer I had who wanted a .5" indent on everything. To set that indent properly requires changing three values for each level. The Text Indent value is for how much the second line of text will be indented. The Aligned At value is for where the numbered value itself will be indented. And the Add Tab Stop At checkbox and value lets you set where the first line of text starts.

So here's what the settings would need to be for the third line of my list in order to get that result you see in the preview up top:

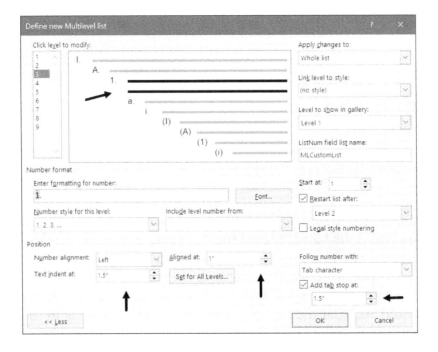

And...Going through all of that to create a custom list works. With one slight flaw.

Which is that it is no longer built to assume that if you hit enter after any numbered line that you will want text instead of another numbered entry. It acts like a numbered or bulleted list and provides the next number by default.

But to get the right spacing and formatting, that is a trade-off I'm willing to make.

One other quick point about this whole custom list process. A few times when I was creating my custom multilevel list I hit enter and it closed out the dialogue box on me even though I wasn't done.

The nice thing is that you can bring up the box again by choosing Define New Multilevel List from that dropdown and your settings will still be there. You do not have to start over if you do accidentally close the dialogue box too soon..

Ultimately, with all those settings here's what I ended up with:

I.	Introduction		
	Some introductory text before we get started		
A.	Point 1		
	1.	Subpoint 1	
		a.	Sub-Subpoint 1
			Explanation of sub-subpoint 1 in far more detail.
	2.	Subpoint 2	
		a.	Sub-Subpoint 1
		b.	Sub-Subpoint 1
B.	Point 2		
	1.	Subpoint 1	
	2.	Subpoint 2	

If I were using this in a real document, I would try to get in my list structure first before I went back and added the text under each point like I have here under Introduction and the first Sub-Subpoint 1.

This was not easy to build. If there is any way to use one of the defaults, do that. And if you're a fancy company that insists on your own custom list numbering and format, save yourself hundreds of thousands of dollars a year and find a way to build it once and then deploy it to all your employees as a template.

Conclusion

Alright, so that was the basics of lists in Word 2019. If you get stuck, reach out and I'm happy to help if I can. I don't check email every day, but I do check it regularly.

Good luck with it.

And if you decide that you want to learn more about Microsoft Word or Word 2019, feel free to check out my other books.

Appendix A: Basic Terminology

Below are some basic terms that I use throughout this guide.

Tab

I refer to the menu choices at the top of the screen (File, Home, Insert, Design, Layout, References, Mailings, Review, View, and Help) as tabs.

Click

If I tell you to click on something, that means to use your mouse (or trackpad) to move the arrow on the screen over to a specific location and left-click or right-click on the option. If I don't specify which to use, left-click.

Select or Highlight

If I tell you to select text, that means to highlight that text either by using your mouse or the arrow and shift keys. Selected text is highlighted in gray.

Dropdown Menu

A dropdown menu provides you a list of choices to select from. There are dropdown menus when you right-click in your document workspace as well as for some of the options listed under the tabs at the top of the screen. Each option with a small arrow next to it will have a dropdown menu available.

Expansion Arrows

I refer to the little arrows at the bottom right corner of most of the sections in each tab as expansion arrows. For example, click on the expansion arrow in the Clipboard section of the Home tab and it will open the Clipboard task pane.

Dialogue Box

Dialogue boxes are pop-up boxes that cover specialized settings. They allow the most granular level of control over an option.

Scroll Bar

Scroll bars are on the right-hand side of the workspace and sometimes along the bottom. They allow you to scroll through your document if your text takes up more space than you can see in the workspace.

Arrow

If I ever tell you to arrow to the left or right or up or down, that just means use your arrow keys.

Task Pane

I refer to the panes that sometimes appear to the left, right, and bottom of the main workspace as task panes. By default you should see the Navigation task pane on the left-hand side when you open a new document in Word.

Control Shortcut

I'll occasionally mention control shortcuts that you can use to perform tasks. When I reference them I'll do so by writing it as Ctrl + a capital letter. For example, Save is Ctrl + S.

   To use one, hold down the Ctrl key and the letter at the same time.

ABOUT THE AUTHOR

M.L. Humphrey is a former stockbroker with a degree in Economics from Stanford and an MBA from Wharton who has spent close to twenty years as a regulator and consultant in the financial services industry.

You can reach M.L. Humphrey at:

mlhumphreywriter@gmail.com

or at

www.mlhumphrey.com

www.ingramcontent.com/pod-product-compliance
Lightning Source LLC
Chambersburg PA
CBHW060513060326
40689CB00020B/4723